Who Are You?

A Guide to Help Adolescents Navigate Through the Social and Emotional Issues of Life

Table of Contents

Introduction

In the era of the "microwave generation", goal setting is not a significant priority. Our youth make decisions about how they will live their lives based on the images they see on TV, the internet, and on social media. They make the decision with no idea how they will achieve this lifestyle, but they expect it to come to fruition at all costs. What they fail to realize is that each doctor they see driving a nice car, every fireman and policeman they see patrolling their neighborhoods, celebrities they listen to on the radio, watch on the internet and TV, or follow on social media followed a plan to get to where they are.

When asked, "What do you want to be when you grow up?" many children respond with careers such as doctor, lawyer, policeman, fireman, nurse, professional athlete, entertainer, rapper, or more recently, reality TV star. Their answers demonstrate that they have decided they are going to be just like the successful people they see driving those nice cars, living in those big houses, and wearing those nice clothes, but they have no idea whatsoever how those people attained their success.

Now I am not saying that success and fame are not attainable, but mega success is not attained by happenstance. One has to set goals and put a plan of action in place if they are serious about their success in life. It was the great Benjamin Franklin that said, "If you fail to plan, you plan to fail." This quote can be counted as truth. One must know where they are going before they start their journey or they will just walk and walk and walk until they either reach their destination by chance or change course all together. Time stops for no one; it is precious. Setting goals and understanding what goes into accomplishing them is more important than ever.

On the other hand, don't think that just because you have set goals and made a plan, that it will always come together. One must know their self-worth, possess character, and have a vision in place for their life. Even though it may seem as though stars like Beyoncé, Kim Kardashian, or LeBron James achieved their success on their own, they needed a lot of support in the early days. They had to convince their family, friends, and even members of their community to take a chance and believe in them before they became the mega stars they are today. Each star that you see needed support from someone who possessed the means to elevate them to celebrity status.

Take a moment and think about yourself. If you had to promote yourself, how would you do it?

Lesson One: Self-Worth

- What is self-worth and who defines it?
- How do I maintain my self-worth regardless of my environment and what the media says?
- I know my self-worth and no one can change my mind.

Lesson 1.1 Who Are You?

How does your self~worth help determine who you are?

Name _____ Date _____

Directions: Define the following key vocabulary terms in your own words based on your personal background knowledge. Use the title of the lesson to help you define the words.

Definitions Quick Write:

Role Models-

Character Traits-

Value-

Directions: Read over the following Essential Question below. In your own words explain what you feel the Essential Question is asking or any personal connections you make with the Essential Question.

Essential Question: How do your role models help define you?

Essential Question Reflection:

SHARED READING

Self-Worth

How many times have you looked in the mirror and wondered about yourself? Why do you look a certain way? Why do you live in a certain place? Why do you dress a certain way? You may even question the way your parents provide for you compared to other people.

Even though you do not have the answers to those questions, you begin to judge yourself based on what others say is truth. You begin to think you are unattractive or ugly because your hair is not a certain texture or length, you don't possess a particular athletic ability, you are not as smart as some of your peers, or wear the latest fashions. You begin to think you are worthless because you don't live in a big house and your parents don't drive a luxury car. You can't seem to understand why anyone would want to be your friend or hang out with you. You begin to doubt your worth based on how you look, live, and dress compared to celebrities who can afford the latest trends and fashions by the world's top designers. You haven't quite realized that how you look, what you wear, or what you or your parents drive has nothing to do with your self- worth.

What did you say to yourself when you woke up this morning? Did you remind yourself that you have the ugliest freckles you have ever seen? Did you tell yourself that no one will even notice you or your new outfit today? Did you remind yourself you are dumb because you failed your last math test? What did you say?

What if you started each day by telling yourself how smart you are? What if you started each day celebrating what makes you an individual even if it happens to be your freckles? What if you reminded yourself how much you like your outfit regardless of what others say? Just what if.

Have you ever thought that it may be your own self-talk that ruins your self-worth? Have you ever stopped to think how different you would feel about yourself if you began each day reminding yourself that you are special? You are unique. You are an individual, and it's okay to go against the crowd. You are smart and can do anything you put your mind to. You will be successful in life.

Take a minute and think about your favorite celebrity, reality star, or athlete. If you took away their money, their status, their clothes, house and car, what would they be left with? They would be left with themselves. The material possessions that we value so much can be a temporary part of life, but the way we think and feel about ourselves is forever.

Who Am I?

Take a moment and think about yourself. Think about your likes, dislikes, hopes, and dreams. What things bring value to you? Are you really satisfied with you? Now think about what you see and hear that changes how you see yourself? Do you look at others' social media posts and wish that was your life? Do you look at the latest reality shows and wonder if you could become famous? Do you watch sports and desire to be the next big athlete? Now answer this: Are you willing to change who you are in order to gain status and material possessions? Read and answer the following questions about yourself.

I describe myself as being _____

_____

_____

_____.

I really value_____ about me because _____

_____

_____

_____.

If I could change one thing about myself, it would be_____

_____

_____.

I would make this change because_____

_____

_____

_____.

I wish others knew _____

_____

_____

_____

_____.

Name _____ Date _____

Who Do I Look Up To?

Have you ever taken the time to think about who your role models (people you look up to) are? It does not have to be just one person. You could admire different qualities about different people for different reasons. Do you know that we sometimes try to imitate or copy the actions, attitudes, and styles of the people we admire? In this lesson, you are going to answer questions about your role models. You may have more than one role model and that's okay. If you do not have a role model in any of the categories below, just leave the section blank.

My Family

My family role model is _____

The thing I admire the most is _____

Describe their:

Style

Attitude

What makes them who they are?

If you could tell them anything it would be…

Sum up in three sentences or less why you consider them a role model.

Name _____ **Date** _____

My Community

My community role model is _____.

The thing I admire the most is _____.

Describe their:

Style

Attitude

What makes them who they are?

If you could tell them anything it would be…

Sum up in three sentences or less why you consider them a role model.

Role Model Continued

Name _____ **Date** _____

My Friends

My friend that is a role model to me is_____.

The thing I admire the most is _____.

Describe their:

Style

Attitude

What makes them who they are?

If you could tell them anything it would be…

Sum up in three sentences or less why you consider them a role model.

Role Model Continued

Name _____ **Date** _____

My Favorite Celebrity

The celebrity that is a role model to me is_____.

The thing I admire the most is _____.

Describe their:

Style

Attitude

What makes them who they are?

If you could tell them anything it would be…

Sum up in three sentences or less why you consider them a role model.

Role Model Continued

Now take a moment and think about the responses you have written about each of your role models. Now take a moment and think about yourself. What trait, if any, do you get from each of your role models? Are there attitudes or styles that you try to mimic? Do you mimic your role model and not even realize it? Take a moment and answer the following reflection questions to end the lesson.

Directions: Read and answer the following questions below.

1. Which of your role model's personality is closest to your own personality? _____

_____Why? _____

_____

2. Which of your role model's style do you admire the most? _____

_____Why?_____

_____

3. Which of your role model's attitude is closet to yours? _____

_____. In what ways are your attitudes similar? _____

_____

_____

4. Are there any other qualities that you get from any of your role models that are not listed? If so, list and explain them below. _____

_____

_____

Lesson 1.2
Self- Worth and Friendships

How does your self-worth impact your friendships?

Name _____ **Date** _____

Directions: Define the following key vocabulary terms in your own words based on your personal background knowledge. Use the title of the lesson to help you define the words.

Definitions Quick Write:

Friendship-

Ideal-

Character Traits-

Directions: Read over the following Essential Question below. In your own words explain what you feel the Essential Question is asking or any personal connections you make with the Essential Question.

Essential Question: What role does self-worth play when selecting friends?

Essential Question Reflection:

Shared Reading

Self- Worth and Friendships

People are social creatures, so it is natural to want to have friends and lots of them. In some instances, people determine their self-worth by the friends they have. If you hang out with the most popular people in your school or neighborhood, you are considered cool or with the "in crowd". Why is it that we are judged by the friends we have, whether good or bad? Do other people really determine who we are as a person? Do we even judge ourselves based on the friends we make, the parties we are invited to, the people we eat lunch with? The answer is yes, we do. If you desire to be in the popular crowd but you are not invited into their circle, you might have the tendency to question yourself and wonder what it is about you that keeps you out of the "in crowd". You may even try to make adjustments in your behavior, such as the way you dress or talk, just to fit in. But what happens if you do all those things and still are not allowed to hang in the popular crowd's circle? Would you be down on yourself? Would you blame the way you look and dress? Would you even blame your parents for not being accepted into their circle?

Now that you have taken the opportunity to think about yourself, think about your friends and the company you keep. Read the questions below and circle the best response.

Do your friends truly reflect you?	**Yes**	**No**	**Not Sure**
Are your friends encouraging you to be the best you can be?	**Yes**	**No**	**Not Sure**
Do your friends appreciate you as a person?	**Yes**	**No**	**Not Sure**
If you were trying to reach a goal, would your friends cheer you on?			
	Yes	**No**	**Not Sure**
Do your friends say nice things about you when you are not around?			
	Yes	**No**	**Not Sure**
Do your parent(s) approve of your friend(s)?	**Yes**	**No**	**Not Sure**

Look at your responses to the questions above. If you marked no 2 or more times, you may want to rethink who you call a "friend". If you marked yes 4 times or more, it looks as if you have a real friend indeed.

Directions: Using the word list on the next page, cut out the character traits that describe you, your best friend, or your ideal friend and paste them in the chart below. If you and your best friend share a specific character trait, cut it out and paste it in the column labeled both.

Me and My Best Friend

Me	Both Me &My Best Friend	My Best Friend	My Ideal Friend

Character Trait Word Bank

bossy	kind	funny	calm
shy	loud	hard working	lazy
moody	selfish	patient	fair
sweet	mean	responsible	trustworthy
brave	nervous	spoiled	smart
hyper	boring	considerate	sensitive
honest	mature	rude	dumb
caring	serious	silly	independent

Lesson 1.3: Television, Radio, Internet, and Social Media

How does television, radio, the internet, and social media affect your self-worth?

Name _____ Date _____

Directions: Define the following key vocabulary terms in your own words based on your personal background knowledge. Use the title of the lesson to help you define the words.

Definitions Quick Write:

Social Media-

Photoshop-

Subconscious-

Directions: Read over the following Essential Question below. In your own words explain what you feel the Essential Question is asking or any personal connections you make with the Essential Question.

Essential Question: How does what I watch on television and the internet, listen to on the radio, and my interaction with social media help shape my self-worth?

Essential Question Reflection:

Shared Reading

Television, Internet, Radio, and Social Media

If you were to take cues from the television, internet, radio, or even social media, your self-worth comes from what you are wearing, who you associate with, what type of music you listen to, and even the type of car you are driving. In this digital age it appears that everyone who is anyone can help shape your worth by what they post about their "everyday" lives. People are quick to post pictures that show you the stacks of money they have, even it is simply their cashed paycheck. They are happy to post pictures of themselves hanging out with the most famous celebrities at parties or clubs. They are quick to point out what car they are driving, even if it is a rental. They even show themselves shopping on a daily basis even if they have not paid one single bill or bought any groceries for their home. They do all this for the admiration, status, and attention they receive from people who follow them.

Most people say they use the internet as a way to keep up with family and friends, but is that truly their motive? I would venture to say that most people use the internet as a way to boost their personal self-worth by using the things they post to solicit responses from people they barely know.

Think about the following questions.

- Do you feel like you are worth more when you post something on the internet and get hundreds of likes? Does it bother you when not one single person likes what you post?
- Do you check the gossip websites every day to see the latest celebrity news?
- Are you constantly checking your Instagram, Twitter, Facebook, etc. to see if anyone has responded to anything you have uploaded?
- Are your favorite television shows "reality" formatted starring your favorite celebrities?
- Are you looking for the latest YouTube videos?
- Do you constantly check what your favorite celebrities are doing and try to imitate the way they dress or act?
- Can you truly say that you are your own person despite the images, advertisements, and celebrities you see?

Name _____ **Date** _____

Directions: Read the paragraph below and then answer the questions that follow.

You and your friends have decided that you want to hang out and listen to some music. You get out your device, turn it on and hear your favorite song. **Take a minute and decide what that song is.** You can't help but dance because you love this song!

Answer the following questions about your favorite song.

1. What is the title of your favorite song and who sings it? _____

    _____

2. Have you ever listened to the lyrics of the song or do you just listen to the beat? _____

    _____

3. What do the lyrics make reference to? _____

    _____

4. What type of reaction do you get from peers when you sing or dance to the song? _____

    _____

5. Do you like getting that type of reaction? _____

    _____

6. If your parents really knew what the song was talking about, would they approve of you

    listening to that song? _____

7. Explain why you like the song. _____

    _____

    _____

8. Do you think it is an appropriate song for someone of your age? Explain your answer.__

    _____

    _____

Name _____ **Date** _____

With the TV lineup full of "reality" shows, it is hard to watch anything else. Think about your favorite television show—the show you watch without any interruptions; the show you DVR if you know you're not going to be home to watch. **Pick that one show that is your all-time favorite.** Think about its characters, storylines, language, and intended audience.

Answer the following questions below concerning your favorite TV show.

1. What is the name of your favorite TV show? _____

2. What are the names of the actors in the show? _____

   _____

3. Do you consider any of the actors role models? If so, who? _____

   _____

4. Why do you consider them role models? _____

   _____

   _____

5. Are there any scenes that are inappropriate for someone your age to watch? _____

6. Explain at least one scene that has been inappropriate. _____

   _____

   _____

7. Do you think watching this show affects you in any way (style, attitude, personality, or character)? Explain your answer. _____

   _____

   _____

Take a minute and think about the internet websites that you visit. You can think of anything from YouTube, Facebook, Twitter, Instagram or any gossip websites that exist and answer the following questions.

Directions: Complete the following paragraph by filling in the blanks based on your personal responses.

My favorite website to visit is _____

I like to visit the site because _____

_____

Do you upload pictures or videos to the internet? _____ If yes, complete the rest of the paragraph.

I like to upload my pictures to the internet because_____

_____

_____

I get the most likes or favorites when my pictures_____

_____

_____

Do you post "inspirational" sayings on the internet? _____ If yes, complete the rest of the paragraph.

I feel _____ when people like what I post,

but I feel _____ when I don't get any likes

on what I posted that day.

I try to make sure my posts are _____

so I can _____.

If my parents made me delete all my social media accounts, I would _____

_____ because _____

_____.

Do you watch videos on the internet? _____ If yes, complete the rest of the paragraph.

My favorite videos to watch on the internet are_____
_____.

I watch these videos because _____
_____.

My parents do/do not like me watching those type of videos because _____

_____
_____.

Based on your responses, how much of an influence does your parents have on your internet and social media activity? _____
_____.

Explain why or why not _____
_____
_____.

Reflection Question:

How much of a role does social media and the internet in general determine how and what you think of yourself?

Notes/Reflections _____

_____

_____

_____

_____

_____

_____

_____

_____

_____

_____

_____

_____

_____

_____

_____

_____

_____

Lesson Two:
Goals

- What are goals?
- Why do we set them?
- How do we set them?
- How will we accomplish them?
- What can keep us from accomplishing our goals?

Lesson 2.1 What Are Goals?

What is the purpose of setting goals?

Name _____ **Date** _____

Directions: Define the following key vocabulary terms in your own words based on your personal background knowledge. Use the title of the lesson to help you define the words.

Definitions Quick Write:

Goal-

Achieve-

Short Term Goals-

Long Term Goals-

Directions: Read over the following Essential Question below. In your own words explain what you feel the Essential Question is asking or any personal connections you make with the Essential Question.

Essential Question: Why is it beneficial to set goals and plans to achieve them?

Essential Question Reflection:

Shared Reading

What Are Goals?

What are goals? In simple terms, a goal is something that you decide to do. For example, you could decide that you are going to make an A in math class at least one time this school year. You made this goal because last school year math was your worst subject, but this year you want to make an A at least one time. Now that you have made that decision, what are you going to do about it? Benjamin Franklin said, "If you fail to plan, you plan to fail." Ultimately it is not enough to just create a goal. You must also put a plan in place to accomplish your goal.

It is important to realize that you do not achieve most things by chance. You must map out what you need to do in order to accomplish the things you want to achieve in life.

Let's go back to the math example. If you want to make an A at least one time this school year, what do you need to do in order to achieve this? Take a few minutes and write out three things you would need to do in order to make your A in math class this year.

1. _____

2. _____

3. _____

Now that you have created your plan, turn and talk with your neighbor to compare action steps. Do you and your neighbor have any steps in common? Were there things that you did not think about?

In this module you will learn why it is important to not only set goals, but why making a plan to accomplish your goals are just as important. Your teacher will help you set goals you want to accomplish fairly quickly, but they will also help you set a few goals that will take you some time to achieve. Don't get discouraged if you have never thought about setting goals. Always remember, it is never too late.

Name _____ Date _____

Goals...Are they really important?

Directions: Read and answer the questions below about goals in general.

Why do people set goals?

What is the purpose of goals?

Do you think it is necessary to have a plan for your life?

Directions: Read and answer the following questions below about your approach to goal setting. It's okay if you have not begun setting any goals for yourself. You will have the opportunity in the upcoming lessons to set your own short term and long term goals.

Have you ever set a goal?

Did you accomplish the goal? Why or Why Not?

Why did you set that goal?

Directions: In the blanks below list five things that you want to achieve. You may want to achieve those five things fairly quickly or it may take some time to achieve some of them. You will be referring to this list periodically throughout the next few lessons.

1. _____

2. _____

3. _____

4. _____

5. _____

Lesson 2.2: Short Term Goals

What is a short term goal?

Name _____ **Date** _____

Directions: From your list of five things (in Lesson 2.1), decide which ones can be classified as short term goals and write them on the spaces below. Try to come up with five short term goals you would like to achieve.

Short Term Goals

1. _____

2. _____

3. _____

4. _____

5. _____

Directions: Now that you have decided what you want to achieve, you will now think about the actions steps you must take in order to achieve those goals. It is recommended that you think of at least three steps that you would need to take to achieve each goal.

Short Term Goals and Action Steps

1. Goal: _____
   Action Steps:
   a. _____

   b. _____

   c. _____

   d. _____

   e. _____

2. Goal: _____
   Action Steps:
   a. _____

   b. _____

   c. _____

   d. _____

   e. _____

3. Goal: _____
   Action Steps:
   a. _____

   b. _____

   c. _____

   d. _____

   e. _____

4. Goal: _____
   Action Steps:
   a. _____

   b. _____

   c. _____

   d. _____

   e. _____

5. Goal: _____
   Action Steps:
   a. _____

   b. _____

   c. _____

   d. _____

   e. _____

Directions: Finally, select three of the above short term goals that you will actively work on achieving. These three goals will be your focus and you will record your progress as it relates to the steps you are taking to achieve these three goals. As you achieve the goals, make it a point to replace the achieved goal with something else (a new goal) you would like to accomplish.

Short Term Goals:

1. _____

2. _____

3. _____

Now that you have listed your goals and action steps, brainstorm people who have already accomplished your goal and list them below.

1. _____

2. _____

3. _____

List three people that can help you achieve your goal.

1. _____

2. _____

3. _____

Now that you have completed the first process of setting goals, reflect on how your self-worth could play either a negative role or positive role in helping you achieve your goals. Explain how your self-worth will affect the process of achieving your goals.

_____

_____

_____

Now think about your character. Explain how your character will impact the achievement of your goals.

_____

_____

_____

Lesson 2.3: Long Term Goals

How do I follow through with my long term goals?

Name _____ **Date** _____

Directions: From your list of five things (from Lesson 2.1) decide which ones can be classified as long term goals and write them on the spaces below. Try to come up with three long term goals you would like to achieve.

Long Term Goals

    1. _____

    2. _____

    3. _____

Long Term Goals and Action Steps

    1. Goal: _____
        Action Steps:

            a. _____

            b. _____

            c. _____

            d. _____

            e. _____

    2. Goal: _____
        Action Steps:

            a. _____

            b. _____

            c. _____

            d. _____

            e. _____

3. Goal: _____
   Action Steps:
      a. _____

      b. _____

      c. _____

      d. _____

      e. _____

Directions: Finally, select one long term goal from above that you will actively work on achieving. This goal will be your focus and you will record your progress as it relates to the steps you are taking to achieve this goal. As you make strides and get closer to achieving your goal, make it a point to begin working on achieving another long term goal on your list.

Long Term Goal:
1. _____

Now that you have listed your goals and action steps, brainstorm people who have already accomplished your goal and list them below.

   1. _____

   2. _____

   3. _____

List three people that can help you achieve your goal.

   1. _____

   2. _____

   3. _____

Now that you have completed the first process of setting goals, complete a reflection on how you will actively work on achieving your goals even when it seems like circumstances are not going your way.

Notes/Reflections _____

_____

_____

_____

_____

_____

_____

_____

_____

_____

_____

_____

_____

_____

_____

_____

_____

Lesson Three:
Character Development

- What does it mean to have character?
- Do I possess a desirable or undesirable character?
- What are the six character traits?

Lesson 3.1 What Does It Mean to Have Character?

Do you have a desirable character?

Name _____ **Date** _____

Directions: Take a moment and look at the words below. Based on what you know, give a brief definition of each word. Your teacher will give you a formal definition of the word before the lesson continues.

Character

Character traits

Perception

Desirable

Undesirable

Directions: Read over the following Essential Question below. In your own words explain what you feel the Essential Question is asking or any personal connections you make with the Essential Question.

Essential Question: What role does a desirable character play in helping you achieve your goals?

Essential Question Reflection:

Shared Reading

Character: Do I really know what that means?

John Wooden once said, "The true test of a man's character is what he does when no one is watching."

Looking at the quote above, take a minute and think about what it is saying. Now take a couple of minutes and explain in your own words what John Wooden was saying about character.

_____
_____
_____

At your teacher's direction, discuss your response with the person beside you or at your table. How similar was your response to other students?

Based on your personal response, do you have the "character" that John Wooden is referencing? Take a moment and read over the following questions and think about how you would answer them based upon your own personal character.

- ✓ Are you a person who is going to do the right thing even if doing the wrong thing would be easier?
- ✓ Will you do what is right because it is right?
- ✓ Will you be the person who would not take advantage of a situation even if you could get away with it; or are you the person who will do anything to get out of a bad situation even when you know you are not being honest?
- ✓ Do you take advantage of the kindness of others for your personal gain and benefit?
- ✓ Does it bother you when you don't keep your word?
- ✓ Would you describe yourself as being a respectful person even to the stranger that you have no connection to?
- ✓ Do you like to do things for people in your community?

Your honest responses to the above reflection questions reveal a lot about your character. Although you are not being asked to respond orally to the questions, just take a moment and look over them and think about yourself. Based on how you would answer those questions, are you a person whom you would be proud to know?

As you work through this lesson, take every opportunity to examine your character and its flaws.

Name _____ **Date** _____

Directions: Along with group mates you will be brainstorming as many words that fit under the categories "Desirable Character Traits" and "Undesirable Character Traits". As you think of a word, write it in the appropriate column. As your teacher reviews the activity with the class, add any words that you do not have in its applicable column for future reference.

Desirable Character Traits　　　　**Undesirable Character Traits**

Name _____ Date _____

"How My Peers See Me"

Traits I Agree With   Traits I Disagree With

What character traits do you think describe you? Use descriptive words or phrases only.

Reflection Questions

1. How did you feel after reading your classmate's responses concerning your character?

2. Why do you think they used certain words or phrases to describe you?

3. How do you want others to view you?

4. What could you do to change their perception of you?

Lesson 3.2: Trustworthiness

Can you really be trusted?

Directions: Take a moment and look at the words below. Based on what you know give a brief definition of each word. Your teacher will give you a formal definition of the word before the lesson continues.

Trustworthy-

Betray-

Violate-

Privileged-

Directions: Read over the following Essential Question below. In your own words explain what you feel the Essential Question is asking or any personal connections you make with the Essential Question.

Essential Question: Why is trustworthiness considered an important character trait?

Essential Question Reflection:

Shared Reading

Trustworthiness

Have you ever been on the receiving end of a secret because you were thought to be trusted, but then you told everyone the secret? If you can answer yes to this question, you may be lacking in the department of trustworthiness.

To be trustworthy simply means you can be trusted with privileged information. This type of information is only shared with those who need to know it. The information could vary from topic to topic but does not need to be shared. In a society that now thrives on gaining the advantage by sharing privileged information, being trustworthy is not as valuable as it used to be. Think about it. If we truly trusted our peers would we have a need for locks on our lockers? Would we need to lock our phones when they are not in use? Would we need to use banks to store our money? Would we have to lock up our homes and turn on home security systems?

Take a few moments and discuss the following questions with your partner or as a table group. Once you have discussed the questions, come up with an answer that everyone can agree with to share with the rest of the class.

1. What does it mean to consider a person trustworthy?

2. What makes a person untrustworthy?

3. Can a person be considered trustworthy but lose your trust? How?

4. What would it take to trust someone once they violated your trust?

5. Are you able to trust someone that betrayed someone you may know?

Reflecting on your group discussion are you as trustworthy as you think? Are your friends as trustworthy as you think?

Directions: Read the question below and list as many words or phrases that you associate with trustworthiness.

What words or character traits do you associate with being trustworthy?

Directions:-Look over your list of words and phrases from above. Thinking about your responses, answer the questions below.

Would you consider yourself a trustworthy person? Why?_____

_____

_____

What role does trustworthiness play in you achieving your goals in life?_____

_____

_____

_____

How important is it to be considered trustworthy?_____

_____

_____

How hard is it to regain trust once it is lost?_____

_____

_____

Trustworthiness

Scenarios

Directions: Read over the scenarios below. As a group or independently, answer the questions that follow.

Scenario One: Yesterday during dismissal you noticed that Ms. Jones dropped $50.00 as she was leaving her classroom. You were about to let her know that she lost the money, but a classmate quickly told you to be quiet. The classmate picked up the money and said they would give you a portion of the money. The next day Ms. Jones was upset because she lost some of the money she needed to get her car fixed and now she is in a bind. You want to do the right thing, but you promised your friend you would not say a word. Ms. Jones is your favorite teacher and she is always giving you treats. Every time you see Ms. Jones it bothers you because you know who has the money. What should you do?

Scenario Two: Over the weekend you and your friends decide to go to the mall. You planned on buying a pair of shoes and maybe a shirt. Your friend simply went with no intentions of purchasing anything. While you were in a shop looking for a shirt, you noticed that your friend slipped some merchandise under their clothes and left the store. Your friend was not caught nor did they mention it to you, but you saw the whole incident. What should you do? Should you confront your friend? What if they ask to go to the mall with you next week?

Scenario Three: One of the most popular kids in school is having a party and you received an invite. The problem is their parents are out of town and this party is being held without their knowledge. You know if you tell your mom about the party she will ask to talk to their parents to make sure adults will be present. If your mom finds out that no adults will be there, you will not be allowed to go. But this is the biggest party of the year! You decide to lie to your mom and say you are going over another friend's house to work on a group project. While at the party, the neighbors call the police because they knew the parents were out of town. The police have now made everyone call their parents to pick them up. What do you tell your mom? How do you explain your presence at the party? What consequences, if any, do you think you should receive?

What would you do?

Directions: After reading each of the scenarios from the previous page, answer the following questions.

How would you handle situation one? Why?_____

_____

_____

_____

_____

_____

What if this happened to someone close to you like your mom or aunt?_____

_____

_____

_____

_____

_____

Do you continue to remain friends with the friend who took the money? Why or

why not?_____

_____

_____

_____

_____

How would you handle situation two?_____

_____

_____

_____

_____

How do you feel walking around the mall with someone who has just stolen merchandise from a store?_____

_____

_____

_____

_____

Your friend brags about stealing the merchandise while with you when you return to school the following Monday, and everyone thinks you also steal from stores. You don't like being labeled a thief, so what do you do?_____

_____

_____

_____

_____

Your friend asks you to go back to the mall this weekend. What is your response and why?_____

_____

_____

_____

_____

How do you handle situation three?_____

_____

_____

_____

_____

How does it feel to lose your mom's trust?_____

_____

_____

_____

_____

What steps are you willing to take to regain her trust?_____

_____

_____

_____

_____

_____

_____

Lesson 3.3: Respect

How do you define respect?

Name _____ **Date** _____

Directions: Take a moment and look at the words below. Based on what you know give a brief definition of each word. Your teacher will give you a formal definition of the word before the lesson continues.

Authority-

Desensitized-

Aggressor-

Deescalate-

Directions: Read over the following Essential Question below. In your own words explain what you feel the Essential Question is asking or any personal connections you make with the Essential Question.

Essential Question: Why is respect a character trait?

Essential Question Reflection:

Name _____ Date _____

Directions: Take a moment and read the following statements. Decide if you agree or disagree with the statements and circle the appropriate answer.

Anticipation Guide (Before Research)

Statement	Before	
1. You only give respect to those who earn it.	Agree	Disagree
2. You don't have to respect authority.	Agree	Disagree
3. People only respect those with lots of money.	Agree	Disagree
4. Respect is earned, not learned.	Agree	Disagree
5. Respect does not have anything to do with achieving your goals.	Agree	Disagree

Directions: After researching and discussing the headlines, read the following statements a second time and decide if your opinion on respect has changed. Circle whether you agree or disagree with the statements and circle the appropriate response.

Anticipation Guide (After Research)

Statement	After	
6. You only give respect to those who earn it.	Agree	Disagree
7. You don't have to respect authority.	Agree	Disagree
8. People only respect those with lots of money.	Agree	Disagree
9. Respect is earned, not learned.	Agree	Disagree
10. Respect does not have anything to do with achieving your goals.	Agree	Disagree

What Is the True Meaning of Respect?

Turn on the TV what do you see? Search the web for current trending topics. Take a listen to what topics your favorite radio personality is talking about on their show. If you were to make a list of those topics, you would probably find that they each share a common theme. Most topics that are trending or making news headlines share the common theme of "lack of respect for our fellow man." These stories have become so common that we have become desensitized to them and as such, they seem normal.

Read the following headlines. Without researching them, explain what you think the headline is about.

Headline One

"Resource Officer Slams Unruly Student"

_____

_____

Headline Two

"Student Charged with Assault and Teacher on Leave After Fight Caught on Tape"

_____

_____

Headline Three

"Brutal St. Clair County High School Attack Caught on Video"

_____

_____

Just by looking at the headlines you can infer that an altercation was recorded and uploaded to the internet. Why are incidents recorded and uploaded to the internet shortly after taking place? Do we as a society get some type of satisfaction when we see these types of incidents? Do incidents such as these help build or destroy a respectful culture in our society?

Name _____ **Date** _____

Directions: After finding the following headlines online, use as many sources available to get to the root of the incident. While completing your research, answer the questions that coincide with the headline.

"Resource Officer Slams Unruly Student"

1. Why did this headline make the news? _____
_____
_____

2. What reason did the officer give for slamming the girl? _____
_____
_____

3. What reason did the girl give for refusing to get out of her seat when asked? _____
_____
_____

4. In your opinion, who is at fault? _____
_____
_____

5. What could each party have done differently to prevent this type of outcome? _____
_____
_____

List all sources you used to gather information. Would you consider your sources credible?

Name _____ **Date** _____

Directions: After finding the following headlines online, use as many sources available to get to the root of the incident. While completing your research, answer the questions that coincide with the headline.

"Student Charged with Assault and Teacher on Leave After Fight Caught on Tape"

    1. How many headlines did you find on this topic?_____

                Choose one before answering the next set of questions.

    2. Why did the altercation take place? _____

_____

_____

    3. Who was the aggressor in this situation? _____

_____

    4. How could this situation have been deescalated? _____

_____

_____

    5. What role does respect play in this situation? _____

_____

_____

List all sources you used to gather information. Would you consider your sources credible?

Name _____ **Date** _____

Directions: After finding the following headlines online, use as many sources available to get to the root of the incident. While completing your research, answer the questions that coincide with the headline.

"Brutal St. Clair County High School Attack Caught on Video"

1. Explain what happened in this incident. _____

_____

_____

_____

2. Why do you think this student was treated this way? _____

_____

_____

3. Why did others stand around and do nothing? _____

_____

_____

List all sources you used to gather information. Would you consider your sources credible?

Name _____ **Date** _____

Directions: After reading and participating in a discussion based on "Thank You Ma'am",
answer the following reflection questions independently.

1. What could have been an alternative outcome for the boy in this situation? _____

_____

_____

2. What character traits did the lady possess that the boy did not? _____

_____

_____

3. How did the lady prove to be trustworthy? _____

_____

_____

4. Why did the boy respect her commands even though he was trying to steal from her? ___

_____

_____

5. What lesson do you think the boy learned from this encounter? _____

_____

_____

6. Do you think the boy changed because of this encounter with the lady? _____

_____

_____

7. What if this happened to a woman in your life? Does your perspective of this encounter
   change? _____

_____

Lesson 3.4: Responsibility

How responsible are you?

Name _____ **Date** _____

Directions: Take a moment and look at the words below. Based on what you know give a brief definition of each word. Your teacher will give you a formal definition of the word before the lesson continues.

Responsibility-

Goals-

Short Term Goals-

Long Term Goals-

Action Plan-

Directions: Read over the following Essential Question below. In your own words explain what you feel the Essential Question is asking or any personal connections you make with the Essential Question.

Essential Question: What role does responsibility play in helping you achieve your goals?

Essential Question Reflection:

Would I Consider Myself Responsible?

Circle the appropriate response to the questions below.

Have your parents ever asked you to complete your chores, but you got distracted and completely forgot about them? **Yes   No**

Have you ever forgotten to take the dog outside and it used the bathroom in the house? **Yes   No**

Have you ever forgotten about your homework because you wanted to go outside, play a video game, or text your friends? **Yes   No**

If you answered yes to any of the above questions, ask yourself, "Am I really a responsible person?"

According to the online Webster dictionary, responsibility is defined as "a duty or task that you are required or expected to do." Being responsible means you complete any task that has been assigned to you by a trusted adult in your life, even if it is not your favorite task or even if you had other plans. Remember, being responsible requires you to complete some task even if that task may interrupt your plans to hang with friends, to play video games, or to watch TV.

You will begin to see that being responsible directly relates to you achieving your stated goals in life. Think about it. Look at your goals and the steps it will take to accomplish them. How many of those steps interrupt your leisure time and require you to take some responsibility in completing the task in order to get you closer to your goal? Remember, most things in life do not happen by chance; they happen because you have properly planned and taken responsibility for the tasks that need to be completed in order to accomplish your goals.

Name _____ **Date** _____

Goal Reflection Activity

Go back and look at the short and long term goals you set at the beginning of the program. Review the goals and also the steps needed to complete the goals. Reflect on the amount of time you have spent working on accomplishing your goals. After you have looked over your goals, answer the following questions.

1. Which short terms goals have you completed?
-
-
-

2. Which short term goals are you close to accomplishing?
-
-
-

3. Which short term goals have you not started working towards accomplishing?
-
-
-

4. What has been the difference in the goals you are close to accomplishing and the goals you have not started working towards?

_____

_____

_____

5. Look at your long term goals. Which long term goals have you begun to work towards accomplishing?
-
-
-

6. Which long term goals do you need additional time to prepare for?
-
-
-

Name _____ **Date** _____

Let's reset your goals now that you know that completing the steps is your responsibility. Even if your goals are remaining the same, consider whether or not you need to add or remove steps in order to accomplish your goals.

Short Term Goals and Action Steps

1. _____

    a. _____

    b. _____

    c. _____

    d. _____

    e. _____

2. _____

    a. _____

    b. _____

    c. _____

    d. _____

    e. _____

3. _____

    a. _____

    b. _____

    c. _____

    d. _____

    e. _____

4. _____

    a. _____

    b. _____

    c. _____

    d. _____

    e. _____

5. _____

    a. _____

    b. _____

    c. _____

    d. _____

    e. _____

Long Term Goals and Action Steps

1. _____

    a. _____

    b. _____

    c. _____

    d. _____

    e. _____

2. _____

    a. _____

    b. _____

    c. _____

    d. _____

    e. _____

3. _____

    a. _____

    b. _____

    c. _____

    d. _____

    e. _____

4. _____

    a. _____

    b. _____

    c. _____

    d. _____

    e. _____

5. _____

    a. _____

    b. _____

    c. _____

    d. _____

    e. _____

Lesson 3.5: Fairness

What do you consider fair?

Fairness

Think about the word "fair" and in your own words write down a meaning for the word. If you cannot write an actual definition, write an example or draw a picture.

Review your explanation of fairness and reflect on the following question:

Did your explanation include more than one person being treated the exact same way without factoring in behavior, attitude, or any other actions? Should they be treated the same, whether positive or negative?

Think about this scenario:

You are in a classroom and the teacher asks everyone to stop talking, and only a few students comply with the teacher's request. The teacher once again asks everyone to get quiet and again only a few students (including you) comply with the request. Since the class as a whole does not comply with the teacher's request, the teacher gives the entire class a write-off to complete. Do you think that this was fair?

If you said in your explanation that being fair meant everyone received the same treatment no matter what, are you having second thoughts about your definition of fairness? Fairness does not mean everyone is treated the same, but fairness does mean that everyone receives a consequence that matches their action, whether good or bad. Think about the last time you were rewarded for doing the right thing and someone else received a consequence for not doing the right thing. Would you say that was fair? Fairness simply means to give someone their just reward regardless if that reward is good or bad; it just needs to match the action that has taken place.

Directions: Read over the following Essential Question below. In your own words explain what you feel the Essential Question is asking or any personal connections you make with the Essential Question.

Essential Question: Why is being fair (fairness) considered an important character trait?

Essential Question Reflection:

Fairness Crossword Puzzle

Across

1 Truthfulness and sincerity

3 Not partial or bias

4 An unfavorable opinion formed without thought, reason, or knowledge

5 Honorable in intentions and actions

9 To be free of bias

10 A person who cheats

12 Sound judgement

Down

2 Guilty of dishonest practices

6 To defraud or swindle

7 A particular tendency

8 To adhere to moral and ethical principles

11 The quality of being just

13 The same as

Word Bank

Honesty   Bias   Cheat   Corrupt   Impartial   Equal   Unbias   Integrity
Reasonable   Justice   Prejudice   Honest   Cheater

Directions: After completing the crossword puzzle, choose four words to use in a sentence and illustrate their meaning. Play close attention and make sure to use the word in the correct context.

Write a sentence using a word from the crossword puzzle. Underline the word.	Illustrate the word
Write a sentence using a word from the crossword puzzle. Underline the word.	Illustrate the word

Write a sentence using a word from the crossword puzzle. Underline the word.	Illustrate the word
Write a sentence using a word from the crossword puzzle. Underline the word.	Illustrate the word

Lesson 3.6: Caring

How much do you really care for others?

Directions: Take a moment and look at the words below. Based on what you know, give a brief definition of each word. Your teacher will give you a formal definition of the word before the lesson continues.

Empathy-

Sympathy-

Directions: Read over the following Essential Question below. In your own words explain what you feel the Essential Question is asking or any personal connections you make with the Essential Question.

Essential Question: Why is it important to care about others and their feelings?

Essential Question Reflection:

Caring

Have you ever gotten your feelings hurt and no one seemed to notice or "care"? The character trait of caring is a special one. If you take a look at the other six pillars of character, caring is embedded in each one. Think about it. If you make a decision that you are going to respect another, help your community, treat peers with fairness, be a person who is trustworthy, or even work to accomplish the goals you have set for yourself, you have to care about something or someone other than yourself.

Complete this quick reflection activity before you begin your lesson.

1. **Name three people you truly care about and give one reason why you care about them.**

2. **Name two things you want to do well and why.**

3. **Name one thing you care about and why.**

Directions:
You and your classmates will be reading a play titled "The New Girl". Your teacher will assign roles to the class. Make sure to follow along as your classmates read their parts.

The New Girl

Jasmine has just moved into town and is the new girl at her school. It is now lunch time and she is looking for somewhere to sit. Watch the reaction of longtime friends when they notice Jasmine is eyeing their table.

Characters

Narrator	Carla	Maria
Jasmine	Steve	Luis

Narrator- Jasmine, a new student in school, has made her way through the lunch line and now needs a place to sit. She sees an empty table with other students in her class and begins to walk towards them…

Steve- Hey Carla, isn't that the new girl in our class?

Carla- Yes, and I hope she is not coming to sit with us!

Steve- If she does, let's all get up and move to another table.

Narrator- Steve, Carla, and Luis all laugh while Maria sits looking disturbed by the conversation of her classmates.

Luis- Yeah, let her sit down and then we'll all get up as if she has the cooties!

Narrator- More laughter erupts from the trio.

Maria- I can't believe that you guys are saying these things.

Carla- What? It's just the new girl. It's not like we even know her or anything.

Maria- That's exactly my point. What if you were to move to a new school and your new classmates were talking about you the way you guys are talking about Jasmine?

Steve- If they do, I'll just punch them in the face!

Luis- Yeah, I would just teach them not to say anything else about me, and that'll show them!

Maria- You guys just don't get it!

Narrator- Just then Jasmine arrives at the table.

Jasmine- Do you guys mind if I sit and eat lunch with you?

1. What do you think will happen next? _____
   _____
   _____

2. What should Maria do? _____
   _____
   _____

3. What would you do if you were Maria? _____
   _____
   _____

4. Have you ever been in this type of situation? Explain. _____
   _____
   _____

Reflection Question: How would you have felt or reacted if you were treated the way Jasmine was treated? _____

_____

_____

_____

_____

Lesson 3.7: Citizenship

What does it mean to be a responsible citizen?

Name _____ **Date** _____

Directions: Take a moment and look at the words below. Based on what you know, give a brief definition of each word. Your teacher will give you a formal definition of the word before the lesson continues.

Citizenship-

Community-

Community Service-

Under Served Populations

Directions: Read over the following Essential Question below. In your own words explain what you feel the Essential Question is asking or any personal connections you make with the Essential Question.

Essential Question: How does servicing our community contribute to the character trait of citizenship?

Essential Question Reflection:

Shared Reading

Am I a Good Citizen?

Have you ever wondered what makes the world function? What about your country? Have you ever given any thought to what makes your state or your local community function day to day? It takes the involvement of ordinary people like you to keep a community running smoothly. Of course you need people like the mayor and council members to run your communities, but it also takes the efforts of ordinary citizens to keep your community running.

Can you think of a time where you did something positive in your community? For example, have you ever participated in a school clean-up day? Have you ever collected used coke cans? Has your classroom ever participated in the recycling program? If you answered yes to any of those questions, you too have participated in events that helped your community. When you participate in those types of activities, you are taking part in community service projects. Community service projects are activities that are completed that are for the good of a community, and it does not have to be the community in which you live either.

Let's take a moment and think about a service project that you could complete within your community. This project can take place in your school, your church or synagogue, or your own neighborhood. Who would you want to help? Why would you want to offer help to that group of people? In this lesson, you will have the opportunity to plan out a community service project that you would like to lead. You may not be able to lead the project this year but you will at least understand the steps that go into planning a community service project.

Name _____ **Date** _____

Community Service Project Brainstorming Activity

Directions: Brainstorm areas of need in your community or a community with high needs. You will be writing the basic information for at least two but no more than four needs in the community. You will need to identify the community, their needs, how to help, who will benefit, time frame for completion, and who could assist you in launching and completing the project. Whatever need you identify in (a) should be detailed on all of the blanks labeled (a) and so on. Remember this is a basic brainstorming activity and should not be detailed. You will complete a more detailed plan for the community service project you choose to launch.

Community _____

I.   Needs of the community:
   a. _____
   b. _____
   c. _____
   d. _____

II.   Ways to help the community:
   a. _____
      _____
   b. _____
      _____
   c. _____
      _____
   d. _____
      _____

III.   Who would benefit from the above project?

a. _____

b. _____

c. _____

d. _____

IV.   Time frame for the project:

a. _____

b. _____

c. _____

d. _____

V.   Who can support me with this project?

a. _____

b. _____

c. _____

d. _____

**Additional
Notes**_____

_____

_____

_____

_____

_____

_____

Community Service Project Planning Activity

Directions: Now that you have completed brainstorming your idea, decide which project you would like to research and plan in detail. You will be presenting your final idea and some of its key information to your peers. The goal is to actually perform this project for the good of the community you live in or want to serve.

Community Service Project you will be completing:

_____

_____

Briefly explain why you chose to complete this project.

_____

_____

_____

_____

What would you like to accomplish through this project?

_____

_____

_____

_____

Name _____ Date _____

Community Service Project Planning Document

Community _____

Title of the Project _____

_____

Who will benefit from the project? _____

_____

_____

What is the timeframe of the project? _____

_____

Who can I enlist for help?

    a. _____

    b. _____

    c. _____

Additional Notes:

_____

_____

_____

_____

_____

_____

Name _____ Date _____

Community Service Project Outline

I. _____

_____

    A. _____

    _____

    B. _____

    _____

    C. _____

    _____

    D. _____

    _____

II. _____

_____

    A. _____

    _____

    B. _____

    _____

    C. _____

    _____

    D. _____

    _____

III. _____

_____

    A. _____

    _____

    B. _____

    _____

    C. _____

    _____

    D. _____

    _____

    _____

IV. _____

_____

    A. _____

    _____

    B. _____

    _____

    C. _____

    _____

    D. _____

    _____

    _____

V. _____

_____

    A. _____

    _____

    _____

    B. _____

    _____

    _____

    C. _____

    _____

    _____

    D. _____

    _____

    _____

Additional Notes

_____

_____

_____

_____

_____

_____

Notes/Reflections _____

_____

_____

_____

_____

_____

_____

_____

_____

_____

_____

_____

_____

_____

_____

_____

Lesson Four:
What is a Vision?

- What is a Vision Board?
- Self-Worth and My Vision
- Character and My Vision
- Goals and My Vision

What is a Vision?

"Now is the time to create a vision for your life. Not concerning yourself with your today because you always have the opportunity to change your tomorrow."

- Erica Battle

Have you ever been sitting in your room or in class and you wander off and imagine yourself living out your life dream? It's like the image is so real that you can almost feel it. Then suddenly, you snap out of your daydream smiling because for a moment, you actually saw your life the way you want it, without any interruptions. That image you saw was not just a daydream; it was the vision you have for your life. A vision is what begins the process of setting goals and creating a plan to achieve the goals you set for yourself.

Have you ever wondered why Beyoncé is so successful? She did not achieve mega stardom by accident. If you have had the opportunity to hear any of her interviews, she talks about how she saw her life in the long term. She has discussed her vision for her life on many occasions. From that vision, she set some goals. To achieve those goals, she created a plan, but it didn't stop there. She understood that in order to see her vision come to life, she had to put her plan into action. Beyoncé talks about how her life has unfolded way beyond her wildest dreams, but in order for that to happen, she first had a dream (or a vision) for her life.

Now take a moment and think about yourself. Imagine your life in 20 years. What do you see? If you need to take a moment and close your eyes, do so. Do you have a vision for your life that includes mega stardom? Do you see yourself being the next President of the United States? Can you see yourself discovering a cure for cancer? What do you see for yourself? Does your vision match with your goals?

Read the following quotes below. What message do you get from them?

"Create the highest grandest vision possible for your life, because you become what you believe." – Oprah Winfrey

_____

_____

"Vision is the Art of seeing what is invisible to others." – Jonathan Swift

_____

_____

Name _____ **Date** _____

Directions: In this lesson you will be writing out your vision for your life in detail. You will describe your dream car and home. You will describe your dream job and how you will be supporting your lifestyle. What will your personal style look like and how often do you plan to vacation? Who will be your friends?

My Life's Vision

My Dream Job

_____
_____
_____
_____
_____
_____

My Dream House and Car(s)

_____
_____
_____
_____
_____
_____

My Dream Wardrobe

_____
_____
_____
_____
_____
_____

My Dream Vacation

_____
_____
_____
_____
_____
_____

Name _____ **Date** _____

My Dream Circle of Friends

_____

_____

_____

_____

_____

My Power of Influence

_____

_____

_____

_____

_____

Summarize Your Life Vision (Add any details you would like)

_____

_____

_____

_____

Name _____ **Date** _____

Answer the following reflection questions below.

1. How does creating a vision for your life make you feel?

2. Where do your goals fit into your vision?

3. Do you believe that writing down your vision increases the possibilities of achieving

   your goals?

Directions: Now it is time to illustrate your vision. You do not have to draw an entire scene, but you may want to draw an example of all the things above. This drawing will serve as the blueprint for your vision board in future lessons. Remember, you don't have to have perfect drawings. You only need a clear vision.

Lesson 4.2: Planning My Vision Board

Have you began creating a mental vision for your life?

Shared Reading

Vision Board

A vision board is a compilation of pictures that are used to recreate your personal life vision and goals. Your vision board can be a digital poster or an actual poster board that you can hang in your home to serve as a constant reminder of what you are striving for. Do you really know the purpose of a vision board?

Focus

Creating a vision board allows you the opportunity to focus on your life dreams. When you are creating a vision board, you are not just looking at the materialistic things that come with achieving your dreams, but you are also looking at the path you would take to achieve your goals. Do you need to attend a traditional college to achieve your dreams? Find a picture and put it on your vision board. Do you need to go to trade school and complete an apprenticeship to achieve your goals? Find images that represent this path and put it on your vision board. Think beyond a car, house, clothes, and jewelry and think about all those things that make up your vision so you can focus on making your vision a reality.

Clarity

As you are creating your vision board, you are selecting images that represent the way you see your life unfolding. Find images that are examples of how you want to live. You may want to be wealthy but not necessarily want a yacht. You may want a nice car but it does not have to be a Lamborghini. So think about your vision and select the images that best represent your vision. Do not worry about the images that others select because that is their vision and not yours.

A Visual to Make Daily Confessions

Even after you have:
- ✓ Set your goals
- ✓ Created an action plan
- ✓ Explained your vision in words
- ✓ Illustrated your vision

There will be days when you feel so far removed from your life's vision. You will have times that nothing seems to go right, which allows self-doubt to set in. You may fail a class or not get that internship, which in turn will have you questioning your life vision. It is during those times that you pull out your Vision Board and begin to speak positive affirmations about your life. There will be times that you will have to encourage yourself when things do not go as planned. Your Vision Board should serve as a constant reminder that you have a plan for your life and no matter what road blocks come your way, you can accomplish any goal that you set for yourself.

Your Vision Board should serve as a constant reminder that you are working on accomplishing your life dreams so you can live the lifestyle you have always dreamed about.

Name _____ **Date** _____

Planning Vision Board

Directions: During the planning stage of your Vision Board, you will be determining what images you will be placing on your board. You will also decide the category for the image. You will only decide what images you would like to see on your board at this time. Look at the example below to guide you through this step. You may provide an explanation for the image like the example or you can simply categorize your images. **NOTE: You may want to refer to lesson 4 when planning your Vision Board to decide which images fit your written explanations.**

Image	Category
Dream Car (Mercedes Benz 500)	Goals (My dream car represents me setting and achieving my goals)

Image	Category

Name _____ **Date** _____

Directions: Using the space below, organize your images based on how you want them placed on your board. You will use a tri-fold board to create your Vision Board, so be mindful of space. You may also want to decorate the board with border, letters, and additional decorative items to make your board appealing.

Lesson 4.3: Presenting Your Vision Board

How does presenting your Vision Board help your life vision come to life?

Name _____ **Date** _____

Directions: Define the following key vocabulary terms in your own words based on your personal background knowledge. Use the title of the lesson to help you define the words.

Definitions Quick Write:

Vision-

Vision Board-

Accountability-

Directions: Read over the following Essential Question below. In your own words explain what you feel the Essential Question is asking or any personal connections you make with the Essential Question.

Essential Question: How does presenting your Vision Board to others help you become accountable to the goals you have set for yourself?

Essential Question Reflection:

Name _____ Date _____

How Will You Present Your Vision Board?

Directions: As you prepare to present your Vision Board, use the spaces below to write the information you would like the community to know about you. You can use this information as a reference during presentations as needed.

Self -Introduction: _____

_____

_____

_____

Goals (Short and Long Term): _____

_____

_____

_____

Persons You Have Enlisted for Help: _____

_____

_____

Explanation of Images on Vision Board: _____

_____

_____

_____

Presentation Notes: _____

_____

_____

_____

_____

_____

_____

_____

_____

_____

_____

_____

_____

_____

_____

_____

_____

_____

INDEX

Made in the USA
Coppell, TX
06 June 2020